This journal belongs to

_____

Date: _____

"For I know the plans I have for you." declares the Lord.
"plans to prosper you and not to harm you.
plans to give you hope and a future."

JEREMIAH 29:11 NIV

You are a beloved child of God, precious to Him in every way. As you seek Him, He will show you the mysteries of life and unfold His unique plans for you—a life full of rich blessing and peaceful assurance using the gifts and experiences that have made you who He has created you to be.

Many have their lives planned out. God has a plan too. Sometimes His plan resembles ours. Sometimes it doesn't. But His plan is always bigger and better than anything we can plan for ourselves. He asks us to trust our future, our plans, our every decision to His guidance.

As you make the daily decisions that affect the path of your life, use this journal to keep track of the thoughts, prayers, challenges, and triumphs of the journey. Our prayer is that you will never forget that wherever the path may lead, God is with you.

The Editors

*G*od created us with an overwhelming desire to soar....
He designed us to be tremendously productive
and "to mount up with wings like eagles," realistically
dreaming of what He can do with our potential.

CAROL KENT

*T*hose who hope in the LORD will renew their strength. They will soar on wings like eagles; they will run and not grow weary, they will walk and not be faint.

ISAIAH 40:31 NIV

*G*od's wisdom is always available to help us choose from alternatives we face,
and help us to follow His eternal plan for us.

GLORIA GAITHER

*L*isten...and be wise, and set your heart on the right path.

PROVERBS 23:19 NIV

*D*o well the little things now and then great things
will come to you by and by, asking to be done.

PERSIAN PROVERB

....

....

....

....

....

....

....

....

....

....

....

....

....

....

....

....

....

....

....

....
....
....
....
....
....
....
....
....
....
....
....
....
....
....
....
....
....

*W*ell done, good and faithful servant! You have been faithful
with a few things; I will put you in charge of many things.

MATTHEW 25:21 NIV

*W*e are made to persist. That's how we find out who we are.

Tobias Wolff

*K*eep on asking, and you will receive what you ask for. Keep on seeking, and you will find. Keep on knocking, and the door will be opened to you.

LUKE 11:9 NLT

*T*he secret of life is that all we have
and are is a gift of grace to be shared.

LLOYD JOHN OGILVIE

*M*any people will praise God because...
you freely share with them and with all others.

2 CORINTHIANS 9:13 NCV

*B*eauty is also to be found in a day's work.

Mamie Sypert Burns

*M*y heart rejoiced in all my labor;
And this was my reward.

ECCLESIASTES 2:10 NKJV

*W*e are so preciously loved by God that we cannot
even comprehend it. No created being can ever know
how much and how sweetly and tenderly God loves them.

JULIAN OF NORWICH

I have loved you with an everlasting love;
I have drawn you with unfailing kindness.

JEREMIAH 31:3 NIV

*D*o not dwell upon your inner failings.... Just do this: Bring your soul to the Great Physician—exactly as you are, even and especially at your worst moment.... For it is in such moments that you will most readily sense His healing presence.

TERESA OF AVILA

*T*hen Christ will make his home in your hearts as you trust in him.
Your roots will grow down into God's love and keep you strong.

EPHESIANS 3:17 NLT

Get over the idea that only children should spend their time in study. Be a student so long as you still have something to learn, and this will mean all your life.

HENRY L. DOHERTY

....

....

....

....

....

....

....

....

....

....

....

....

....

....

....

....

....

....

....

*T*each the wise, and they will become even wiser;
teach good people, and they will learn even more.

*R*ecognizing who we are in Christ and aligning our life with God's purpose for us gives a sense of destiny.... It gives form and direction to our life.

JEAN FLEMING

*Y*ou guide me with your counsel, leading me to a glorious destiny.

PSALM 73:24 NLT

*Y*ou learn something every day if you pay attention.

RAY LEBLOND

*P*ay attention to what I say; turn your ear to my words.
Do not let them out of your sight, keep them within your heart.

PROVERBS 4:20–21 NIV

*I*n waiting we begin to get in touch with the rhythms of life—stillness and action, listening and decision. They are the rhythms of God. It is in the everyday and the commonplace that we learn patience, acceptance, and contentment.

RICHARD J. FOSTER

*M*ay he keep us centered and devoted to him, following the life path he has cleared, watching the signposts, walking at the pace and rhythms he laid down for our ancestors.

1 KINGS 8:58 MSG

A span of life is nothing. But the man or woman who lives that span, they are something. They can fill that tiny span with meaning, so its quality is immeasurable, though its quantity may be insignificant.

CHAIM POTOK

I pray that you...will have the power to understand the greatness
of Christ's love—how wide and how long and how high and how deep
that love is.... Then you can be filled with the fullness of God.

EPHESIANS 3:18—19 NCV

*K*ind words are jewels that live in the heart and soul and remain as blessed memories years after they have been spoken.

MARVEA JOHNSON

*K*ind words are like honey—sweet to the soul and healthy for the body.

PROVERBS 16:24 NLT

They are well guided that God guides.

SCOTTISH PROVERB

*W*e can make our plans,
but the LORD determines our steps.

PROVERBS 16:9 NLT

The road to the head lies through the heart.

AMERICAN PROVERB

*T*rust in the LORD with all your heart, and lean not on your own understanding;
In all your ways acknowledge Him, and He shall direct your paths.

PROVERBS 3:5–6 NKJV

*E*veryone has a unique role to fill in the world
and is important in some respect. Everyone,
including and perhaps especially you, is indispensable.

NATHANIEL HAWTHORNE

*J*ust as we have many members in one body and all the members do not have the same function, so we…have gifts that differ according to the grace given to us.

ROMANS 12:4–6 NASB

We learn more by looking for the answer to a question...
than we do from learning the answer itself.

LLOYD ALEXANDER

You will search again for the LORD your God. And if you search
for him with all your heart and soul, you will find him.

DEUTERONOMY 4:29 NLT

*E*ven when all we see are the tangled threads
on the backside of life's tapestry, we know that
God is good and is out to do us good always.

RICHARD J. FOSTER

....

....

....

....

....

....

....

....

....

....

....

....

....

....

....

....

....

....

*W*e know that in everything God works for the good of those who love him. They are the people he called, because that was his plan.

ROMANS 8:28 NCV

*W*hat we feel, think, and do this moment influences both our present and the future in ways we may never know. Begin. Start right where you are. Consider your possibilities and find inspiration...to add more meaning and zest to your life.

ALEXANDRA STODDARD

*C*ommit to the LORD whatever you do, and he will establish your plans.

PROVERBS 16:3 NIV

A woman of beauty...knows in her quiet center
where God dwells that He finds her beautiful,
and deems her worthy, and in Him, she is enough.

JOHN AND STASI ELDREDGE

*C*lothe yourselves...with the beauty that comes from within,
the unfading beauty of a gentle and quiet spirit, which is so precious to God.

1 PETER 3:4 NLT

*T*here is nothing like a dream to create the future.

VICTOR HUGO

*H*ope deferred makes the heart sick, but a dream fulfilled is a tree of life.

PROVERB 13:12 NLT

*S*ociety needs people who...know how
to be compassionate and honest.... You can't run
the society on data and computers alone.

ALVIN TOFFLER

*W*hat happens when we live God's way? He brings gifts into our lives...things like affection for others, exuberance about life...a sense of compassion in the heart, and a conviction that a basic holiness permeates things and people.

GALATIANS 5:22–23 MSG

*G*od has no problems, only plans.

CORRIE TEN BOOM

*T*he plans of the LORD stand firm forever,
the purposes of his heart through all generations.

PSALM 33:11 NIV

*I*nasmuch as anyone pushes you nearer to God,
he or she is your friend.

*I*t is good and pleasant when God's people live together in peace!

PSALM 133:1 NCV

Your future is as bright as the promises of God.

A. JUDSON

No eye has seen, no ear has heard, and no mind has imagined
what God has prepared for those who love him.

1 Corinthians 2:9 NLT

I trust You always, though I may seem to be lost
and in the shadow of death. I will not fear, for You are ever
with me. And You will never leave me to face my perils alone.

THOMAS MERTON

The LORD is my shepherd; I shall not want. He makes me to lie down in green pastures; He leads me beside the still waters. He restores my soul.

PSALM 23:1—3 NKJV

*G*od's love never ceases. Never.... God doesn't love us less if we fail
or more if we succeed. God's love never ceases.

MAX LUCADO

*G*od promises to love me all day,
sing songs all through the night!
My life is God's prayer.

PSALM 42:8 MSG

*G*od cares for the world He created, from the rising
of a nation to the falling of the sparrow. Everything
in the world lies under the watchful gaze of His
providential eyes, from the numbering of the days
of our life to the numbering of the hairs on our head.

KEN GIRE

*L*ook straight ahead, and fix your eyes on what lies before you.
Mark out a straight path for your feet; stay on the safe path.
Don't get sidetracked; keep your feet from following evil.

<small>PROVERBS 4:25—27 NLT</small>

*G*od never abandons anyone on whom He has set His love; nor does Christ,
the good shepherd, ever lose track of His sheep.

J. I. PACKER

*I*f God cares so wonderfully for wildflowers that are here today
and thrown into the fire tomorrow, he will certainly care for you.

MATTHEW 6:30 NLT

*G*od has designs on our future...and He has designed
us for the future. He has given us something
to do in the future that no one else can do.

RUTH SENTER

"*For* I know the plans I have for you," declares the LORD,
"plans to prosper you and not to harm you, plans to give you hope and a future."

JEREMIAH 29:11 NIV

*B*eauty puts a face on God. When we gaze at nature, at a loved one, at a work of art,
our soul immediately recognizes and is drawn to the face of God.

MARGARET BROWNLEY

I will give thanks to You, for I am fearfully and wonderfully made;
Wonderful are Your works, and my soul knows it very well.

PSALM 139:14 NASB

*W*e may not all reach God's ideal for us,
but with His help we may move in that direction
day by day as we relate every detail of our lives to Him.

*F*rom now on every road you travel
Will take you to God.
Follow the Covenant signs;
Read the charted directions.

PSALM 25:10 MSG

*W*hatever God tells us to do, He also helps us to do.

DORA GREENWELL

*T*he Holy Spirit helps us in our weakness. For example, we don't know
what God wants us to pray for. But the Holy Spirit prays for us
with groanings that cannot be expressed in words.

ROMANS 8:26 NLT

*E*very day we live is a priceless gift of God,
loaded with possibilities to learn
something new, to gain fresh insights.

DALE EVANS ROGERS

*T*his is the day the LORD has made;
We will rejoice and be glad in it.

PSALM 118:24 NKJV

Your looks at this age are a gift. You received them from your ancestors.
But if you are still beautiful when your hair is gray
and your bones ache, that beauty is from your own doing.

*M*y cup brims with blessing.
Your beauty and love chase after me every day of my life.

PSALM 23:5–6 MSG

A dream becomes a goal when
action is taken toward its achievement.

BO BENNETT

I focus on this one thing: Forgetting the past and looking forward to what lies ahead, I press on to reach the end of the race and receive the heavenly prize.

PHILIPPIANS 3:13—14 NLT

I would rather walk with God in the dark than go alone in the light.

MARY GARDINER BRAINARD

I will bless the Lord who guides me; even at night my heart instructs me.
I know the Lord is always with me. I will not be shaken, for he is right beside me.

PSALM 16:7–8 NLT

Try to keep your sense of humor! When you can see the funny side of a problem, sometimes it stops being so much of a problem.

EMILIE BARNES

*T*hose who plant in tears
will harvest with shouts of joy.
They weep as they go to plant their seed,
but they sing as they return with the harvest.

Psalm 126:5–6 NLT

*D*on't judge each day by the harvest you reap but by the seeds that you plant.

ROBERT LOUIS STEVENSON

*P*lant your seed in the morning and keep busy all afternoon,
for you don't know if profit will come from one activity or another—or maybe both.

ECCLESIASTES 11:6 NLT

The victory of success is half won when one gains the habit of setting goals and achieving them. Even the most tedious chore will become endurable as you parade through each day convinced that every task, no matter how menial or boring, brings you closer to fulfilling your dreams.

OG MANDINO

*S*eek first God's kingdom and what God wants.
Then all your other needs will be met as well.

MATTHEW 6:33 NCV

*G*od's Word acts as a light for our paths. It can help scare off
unwanted thoughts in our minds and protect us from the enemy.

GARY SMALLEY AND JOHN TRENT

Your word is a lamp for my feet, a light on my path.

PSALM 119:105 NIV

*O*ur Creator would never have made such lovely days,
and given us the deep hearts to enjoy them, above and beyond
all thought, unless we were meant to be immortal.

NATHANIEL HAWTHORNE

*T*he whole earth is full of His glory!

*W*hen the world around us staggers from lack of direction,
God offers purpose, hope, and certainty.

GLORIA GAITHER

*E*verything has already been decided. It was known long ago what each person would be. So there's no use arguing with God about your destiny.

ECCLESIASTES 6:10 NLT

*I*n God's wisdom, He frequently chooses
to meet our needs by showing His love toward us
through the hands and hearts of others.

JACK HAYFORD

....

....

....

....

....

....

....

....

....

....

....

....

....

....

....

....

....

....

....

*U*se your freedom to serve one another in love. For the whole law
can be summed up in this one command: "Love your neighbor as yourself."

GALATIANS 5:13–14 NLT

We do not want merely to see beauty, though, God knows, even that is bounty enough. We want something else which can hardly be put into words—to be united with the beauty we see, to pass into it, to receive it into ourselves.

C. S. LEWIS

I'm asking God for one thing, only one thing:
To live with him in his house my whole life long.
I'll contemplate his beauty; I'll study at his feet.
That's the only quiet, secure place in a noisy world.

PSALM 27:4–5 MSG

Go confidently in the direction of your dreams.
Live the life you have imagined.

HENRY DAVID THOREAU

*T*here is surely a future hope for you, and your hope will not be cut off.

PROVERBS 23:18 NIV

There are high spots in all of our lives, and most of them come about through encouragement from someone else.

GEORGE ADAMS

*E*ncourage one another and build up one another, just as you also are doing.

1 THESSALONIANS 5:11 NASB

God has not promised sun without rain,
Joy without sorrow, peace without pain.
But God has promised strength for the day,
Rest for the labor, light for the way.

ANNIE JOHNSON FLINT

....

....

....

....

....

....

....

....

....

....

....

....

....

....

....

....

....

....

....

....

....

....

....

....

I will lead the blind by ways they have not known,
along unfamiliar paths I will guide them; I will turn the darkness
into light before them and make the rough places smooth.

ISAIAH 42:16 NIV

*G*od never abandons anyone on whom He has set His love;
nor does Christ, the good shepherd, ever lose track of His sheep.

J. I. PACKER

Yea, though I walk through the valley of the shadow of death, I will fear no evil;
for You are with me; Your rod and Your staff, they comfort me.
You prepare a table before me in the presence of my enemies.

PSALM 23:4–5 NKJV

*T*ime is a very precious gift of God; so precious
that it's only given to us moment by moment.

AMELIA BARR

*B*e careful how you live.... Make the most of every opportunity....
Don't act thoughtlessly, but understand what the Lord wants you to do.

EPHESIANS 5:15–17 NLT

*T*ogether we will forge a pathway up the high mountain.... Though the path is difficult and the scenery dull at the moment, there are sparkling surprises just around the bend. Stay on the path [God] has selected for you. It is truly the path of life.

SARAH YOUNG

....

....

....

....

....

....

....

....

....

....

....

....

....

....

....

You will show me the path of life;
In Your presence is fullness of joy;
At Your right hand are pleasures forevermore.

PSALM 16:11 NKJV

It is pleasing to God whenever you rejoice
or laugh from the bottom of your heart.

MARTIN LUTHER

*I*n this world you will have trouble. But take heart! I have overcome the world.

JOHN 16:33 NIV

It's what you learn after you know it all that counts.

HARRY S. TRUMAN

*L*et the wise listen and add to their learning, and let the discerning get guidance.

PROVERBS 1:5 NIV

*D*on't be afraid to take a big step if one is indicated;
you can't cross a chasm in two small jumps.

DAVID LLOYD GEORGE

$\mathcal{M}$ay he give you the power to accomplish all the good things
your faith prompts you to do.

2 THESSALONIANS 1:11 NLT

The price of success is hard work, dedication to the job at hand, and the determination that whether we win or lose, we have applied the best of ourselves to the task at hand.

VINCENT T. LOMBARDI

*M*ay He grant you according to your heart's desire,
And fulfill all your purpose.

PSALM 20:4 NKJV

*B*ecause God is responsible for our welfare, we are told
to cast all our care upon Him, for He cares for us.
God says, "I'll take the burden—don't give it a thought—
leave it to Me." God is keenly aware that we are
dependent upon Him for life's necessities.

BILLY GRAHAM

I lay down and slept,
yet I woke up in safety,
for the LORD was watching over me.

PSALM 3:5 NLT

*G*iving is a joy if we do it in the right spirit. It all depends
on whether we think of it as "What can I spare?" or as "What can I share?"

ESTHER YORK BURKHOLDER

*E*ach of you has received a gift to use to serve others.
Be good servants of God's various gifts of grace.

1 PETER 4:10 NCV

*L*ift up your eyes. Your heavenly Father waits to bless you—in inconceivable ways to make your life what you never dreamed it could be.

ANNE ORTLAND

I will lift up my eyes to the mountains; from where shall my help come?
My help comes from the LORD , who made heaven and earth.

PSALM 121:1—2 NASB

*G*et into the habit of saying, "Speak, Lord," and life will become a romance.

OSWALD CHAMBERS

Nothing in all creation will ever be able to separate us from the love of God.

ROMANS 8:39 NLT

*W*henever it is possible, choose some occupation
which you should do even if you did not need the money.

WILLIAM LYON PHELPS

*D*o your work with enthusiasm. Work as if you were serving the Lord, not as if you were serving only men and women.

EPHESIANS 6:7 NCV

*B*ecoming a leader is synonymous with becoming yourself.
It is precisely that simple, and it is also that difficult.

WARREN G. BENNIS

*A*nyone who belongs to Christ has become a new person.
The old life is gone; a new life has begun! And all of this is a gift from God.

2 CORINTHIANS 5:17—18 NLT

*W*hoever walks toward God one step,
God runs toward him two.

JEWISH PROVERB

*W*e love Him because He first loved us.

1 JOHN 4:19 NKJV

If you have never heard the mountains singing, or seen the trees of the field clapping their hands, do not think because of that they don't. Ask God to open your ears so you may hear it, and your eyes so you may see it, because, though few people ever know it, they do, my friend, they do.

PHILLIPS McCANDLISH

You will go out in joy and be led forth in peace; the mountains and hills will burst into song before you, and all the trees of the field will clap their hands.

ISAIAH 55:12 NIV

The true meaning of life is to plant trees,
under whose shade you do not expect to sit.

NELSON HENDERSON

*I*t's not important who does the planting, or who does the watering. What's important is that God makes the seed grow. The one who plants and the one who waters work together with the same purpose.

1 CORINTHIANS 3:7—8 NLT

*T*oday is unique! It has never occurred before and it will never be repeated. At midnight it will end, quietly, suddenly, totally. Forever. But the hours between now and then are opportunities with eternal possibilities.

CHARLES R. SWINDOLL

*G*o after a life of love as if your life depended on it—because it does.
Give yourselves to the gifts God gives you. Most of all, try to proclaim his truth.

1 CORINTHIANS 14:1 MSG

*T*here never was any heart truly great and generous,
that was not also tender and compassionate.

ROBERT SOUTH

*B*e agreeable, be sympathetic, be loving, be compassionate, be humble....
Bless—that's your job, to bless. You'll be a blessing and also get a blessing.

1 PETER 3:8–9 MSG

Nothing is as real as a dream. The world can change around you, but your dream will not. Responsibilities need not erase it. Duties need not obscure it. Because the dream is within you, no one can take it away.

TOM CLANCY

*E*very good and perfect gift is from above, coming down from the Father
of the heavenly lights, who does not change like shifting shadows.

JAMES 1:17 NIV

*D*o you want to be wise? Choose wise friends.

CHARLES SWINDOLL

A sweet friendship refreshes the soul.

PROVERBS 27:9 MSG

*H*eaven often seems distant and unknown,
but if He who made the road...is our guide, we need not fear to lose the way.

HENRY VAN DYKE

I am always with you; you hold me by my right hand.

PSALM 73:23 NIV

*G*od, who has led you safely on so far, will lead you on to the end. Be altogether at rest in the loving holy confidence which you ought to have in His heavenly providence.

FRANCIS DE SALES

*T*he LORD directs the steps of the godly.
He delights in every detail of their lives.
Though they stumble, they will never fall,
for the LORD holds them by the hand.

PSALM 37:23–24 NLT

A study of the nature and character of God is the most practical project anyone can engage in. Knowing about God is crucially important for the living of our lives.

J. I. PACKER

*C*ontinue in what you have learned and have become convinced of,
because you know those from whom you learned it, and how from infancy
you have known the Holy Scriptures, which are able to make you wise.

2 TIMOTHY 3:14–15 NIV

*G*od is every moment totally aware of each one of us.
Totally aware in intense concentration and love....
No one passes through any area of life, happy or tragic,
without the attention of God with them.

EUGENIA PRICE

The LORD protects those who are loyal to him.

PSALM 31:23 NLT

You can't experience success beyond your wildest dreams
until you dare to dream something wild!

SCOTT SORRELL

*G*od can do anything, you know—far more than you could
ever imagine or guess or request in your wildest dreams!

EPHESIANS 3:20 MSG

*L*ife is not easy for any of us. But what of that?
We must have perseverance and above all confidence
in ourselves. We must believe that we are gifted
for something and that this thing must be attained.

MARIE CURIE

God blesses those who patiently endure testing and temptation. Afterward
they will receive the crown of life that God has promised to those who love him.

JAMES 1:12 NLT

*O*ur greatness rests solely on the fact that God in His incomprehensible goodness has bestowed His love upon us. God does not love us because we are so valuable; we are valuable because God loves us.

HELMUT THIELICKE

*For the Lord is good and his love endures forever;
his faithfulness continues through all generations.*

PSALM 100:5 NIV

*T*he measure of a life, after all,
is not its duration but its donation.

CORRIE TEN BOOM

....

....

....

....

....

....

....

....

....

....

....

....

....

....

....

....

....

....

Give, and it will be given to you. A good measure, pressed down,
shaken together and running over, will be poured into your lap.
For with the measure you use, it will be measured to you.

LUKE 6:38 NIV

*T*here are no shortcuts to any place worth going.

BEVERLY SILLS

We are merely moving shadows,
and all our busy rushing ends in nothing....
And so, Lord, where do I put my hope?
My only hope is in you.

PSALM 39:6–7 NLT

Ellie Claire® Gift & Paper Expressions
Franklin, TN 37067
EllieClaire.com
Ellie Claire is a registered trademark of Worthy Media, Inc.

For I Know the Plans... Classic Journal
© 2015 Ellie Claire Gift & Paper Expressions
Published by Ellie Claire, an imprint of Worthy Publishing Group,
a division of Worthy Media, Inc.

ISBN 978-1-63326-052-8

Excluding Scripture verses, references to men and masculine pronouns have been replaced with
gender-neutral references.

Stock or custom editions of Ellie Claire titles may be purchased in bulk for educational,
business, ministry, fundraising, or sales promotional use. For information, please email
info@EllieClaire.com.

Compiled by Marilyn Jansen
Designed by Melissa Reagan

Printed in China
3 4 5 6 7 8 9 10 11 – 20 19 18 17 16 15